Cosmic Grooves:

Pisces

Cosmic Grooves:

Pisces

by Jane Hodges

CHRONICLE BOOKS
SAN FRANCISCO

RHINO

Text copyright © 2001 Chronicle Books LLC
Executive Producer: Andrea Kinloch
Compilation Produced for Release: Dave Kapp, Mark Pinkus, and Andrea Kinloch
Remastering: Bob Fisher at Pacific Multimedia Corp.
Licensing: Wendi Cartwright
Project Assistance: Patrick Milligan, Amy Utstein, Mary Patton, and Mason Williams

Rhino Entertainment Company
10635 Santa Monica Blvd.
Los Angeles, California 90025
www.rhino.com

Library of Congress Cataloging-in-Publication Data available.
ISBN 0-8118-3069-1

Printed in China

Designed by Michael Mabry
Illustration copyright © 2001 Michael Mabry

Distributed in Canada by Raincoast Books
9050 Shaughnessy Street
Vancouver, British Columbia V6P 6E5

10 9 8 7 6 5 4 3 2 1

Chronicle Books LLC
85 Second Street
San Francisco, California 94105
www.chroniclebooks.com

Pisces

February 21 to March 20

Element: *Water*

Quality: *Mutable, a sign that adapts*

Motto: *"I believe"*

Planetary Ruler: ♆ *Neptune, the planet of illusion and fantasy*

Neptune's Influence: *The influence of Neptune makes Pisces the most imaginative sign in the zodiac. Spiritual individuals born under this sign believe only the best about their friends and loved ones. Their blind faith influences others to become better people. The downside of their creativity is that Pisceans are capable of deceiving themselves or not seeing reality fully. However, when their dreams do come true, life seems full of beauty and possibilities, and expressive Pisceans share their joy and inspire those around them.*

Symbol: *Fish*

Fish's Influence: *Pisces is one of the most selfless signs, and its symbol—two connected fish trying to swim in opposite directions—indicates that Fish folks struggle with their sensitive emotions. These idealistic people can exult in life one day and suffer disillusionment the next, when they discover they've been putting faith in mere fantasy. Pisceans may sometimes live in a dream world and avoid reality, but ultimately they find a way to live in the real world while also experiencing the beauty of their imaginations.*

How to recognize a Pisces: *
*Expressive eyes, languid
sensuality, light step*
Pick–up line: *"Am I dreaming
or are you for real?"*

What a Pisces wants: *
Compassion, romance
What a Pisces needs:
Discipline, resilience
Jukebox selection: *"Lean on Me"*

Introducing Pisces

Ruled by Neptune Ψ, the planet that cultivates imagination and fantasy, Pisceans are the zodiac's artists and spiritualists. They spend their life searching for what may seem ephemeral to others: creative fulfillment, inner peace, and unconditional love with a soulmate. Pisces is one of the least materialistic, ego-driven signs in the zodiac, and is governed by a quiet and gentle energy. Pisceans absorb the emotional environment around them and attempt to connect and empathize with everyone they encounter. Their intuition is superb, and they are comfortable listening to and discussing their unconscious urges, vivid dreams, and creativity. Pisceans believe they can make a difference by helping others. They are capable of great joy and faith, but often their faith is tested by periods of doubt and even depression.

Pisces kids are dreamy and imaginative, and will spend delightful hours making and sharing art with others. Because they are so sensitive, parents will need to introduce them to real-world responsibilities carefully without shattering their fantasy life. When young, they are romantic and easily hurt. While some

Pisceans are shy, most spend their youth pursuing, then recovering from, dramatic relationships. As teens, they need to learn to set boundaries with others who may occasionally take advantage of their generosity and empathetic ear. In adulthood, it is important that Pisceans find a way to balance their responsibilities to their career and their loved ones with their responsibilities to their spiritual beliefs. It is essential they find professional or marital partners who can help them temper this tendency—people who can help them stay clear about their own needs and get those needs met.

In their spare time, Pisceans enjoy creative and spiritual pursuits. They often need to get away from others to center or quiet their thoughts, so meditation, yoga, or long walks near water appeal to them. Some Pisceans are completely capable of living alone, especially as artists or members of a religious order. Excellent gardeners, their nurturing touch can yield delightful fresh vegetables and herbs. They are frequently outstanding cooks as well. Since Neptune rules imagery and illusion, Pisceans enjoy creating visual art or collecting photography, paintings, and films. Pisceans often do volunteer work and are excellent with children, to whom they relate effortlessly and imaginatively. Life, to Pisces, is about unselfish love—and finding and nourishing those who are truly ready to accept it.

Dedicated to Pisces

Pisceans like music that heightens their many moods. The right tunes can soothe fears while reminding that imagination is the key to happiness.

Devoted
: Pisceans genuinely care about others' problems and generously offer their support to anyone in need. *I Say a Little Prayer* sung by Aretha Franklin sums up their selfless approach.

Compassionate
: During tough times, empathetic Fish folks can be the best friends around, and *Lean on Me* performed by Club Nouveau celebrates the depth of Pisces relationships.

Mysterious
: Enigmatic Pisceans are surrounded by a seductive aura other find appealing—and *I Keep You Guessing* by Ike & Tina Turner describes their ability to attract admirers.

Empathetic
: No matter what's happening in their own lives, Fish folks will drop everything to lend a hand. *I Can Help* sung by Jo-El Sonnier could be the theme song for Piscean volunteerism and empathy.

Sensitive
: Vulnerable Pisceans buckle under criticism and unkindness. *Try a Little Tenderness* sung by Otis Redding is an apt reminder that they should be treated with the same compassion they bestow on others.

Escapist	Pisceans have trouble separating reality from daydream, and *World of Contradictions* by Johnny Winter reveals what happens when they take off their rose-colored glasses.
Forgiving	Though others may take advantage of Fish folks, accepting Pisceans forgive and forget. *All Is Forgiven* by Jellyfish celebrates their ability to turn the other cheek.
Appreciative	Pisceans rarely take others for granted, and *Thank You for Being a Friend* by Andrew Gold expresses the acknowledgment Fish folks offer the people they trust.
Imaginative	Flights of fancy come naturally to Pisceans, and *Daydream* by The Lovin' Spoonful captures the ease with which this sign finds inspiration in daily life.
Trusting	Dreamy Fish folks believe love is magical, but they need a practical partner, as Shelley Fabares illustrates in *I Know You'll Be There*.
Loyal	Pisceans love and accept others unconditionally and *Count on Me* by Jefferson Starship celebrates this sign's commitment to friends.
Spiritual	From creative and escapist to isolated and detached, the archetypes of the Pisces persona are mythologized in *Pisces* by Cannonball Adderley.

Pisces at Work

Ruled by a water sign, Pisceans follow hunches and gut instincts. Many work well in healing professions or in the arts, since solitary work and dealing with deep emotions comes naturally to them. In an office, their best traits are adaptability and intuition, and they can often predict market trends and handle business travel with ease. Pisceans need to feel needed more than they desire major financial reward. Providing behind-the-scenes support or working solo within a group practice appeals to them, since they don't like the limelight but do enjoy contributing to a group enterprise. Rather than grapple for the brass name plate, these individuals genuinely want to set an example for others, even in competitive circumstances. While they are often self-deprecating, their commitment to their work often earns them the top job in a corporate setting. Pisceans can successfully manage highly complex and diversified companies. Their ability to envision all possible outcomes of any business deal, and to create imaginative new products or companies, can make them very effective leaders.

Pisces Careers

Pisceans are born artists, healers, and empathizers. Jobs where they must respond to and interpret emotions appeal to them. Many can accept the professional artist's fluctuating lifestyle in exchange for the rewards of doing what they love for a living. This sign, strong with visual imagery, is at home in the world of film and television, so many Fish folks write or produce for the screen. Their empathy makes them talented poets, academics, and storytellers. Their natural rapport with youngsters, as exemplified by beloved Pisces children's writer Dr. Seuss, makes them great elementary school teachers, or executives in children's media. Other Pisceans choose careers like psychology, ministry, or social work, and innately know how to draw others out of their shells. Adaptive and curious, those born under this sign can succeed in field research or journalism. Pisceans Paula Zahn and Sam Donaldson found success as television interviewers. Such skills, on a more abstract level, work well in careers that involve marketing research or economic forecasting. Like Pisces media giant Rupert Murdoch, many Fish folks succeed at running large, diversified companies.

Pisces in Love

Wistful Pisceans live for romance—before, between, and during committed relationships. They believe their soulmate is out there, and Pisceans will go through many turbulent relationships until they feel a spiritual connection to a partner. Those born under this dreamy sign attract the opposite sex easily, but must guard against taking up with needy people who will abuse their inherent compassion. While Pisceans want a fairy-tale romance filled with spontaneous trips to faraway places, long days of lovemaking, and delightful surprises, what they need is a partner who anchors this fantasy in reality. While their emotions are volatile at times, especially when they grow disillusioned, they naturally create relationships characterized by romance and gentle kindness. If they are wise enough—or lucky enough—to find a supportive, stable partner and strike a balance between fantasy and reality, they can enjoy a life of sustained creativity and romance.

Pisces Relationships

Pisces & Aries (*March 21 to April 20*)   Harmonious

Pisces & Taurus (*April 21 to May 21*)   Passionate

Pisces & Gemini (*May 22 to June 21*)   Challenging

Pisces & Cancer (*June 22 to July 22*)   Passionate

Pisces & Leo (*July 23 to August 23*)   Challenging

Pisces & Virgo (*August 24 to September 22*)   Passionate

Pisces & Libra (*September 23 to October 23*)   Challenging

Pisces & Scorpio (*October 24 to November 22*)   Passionate

Pisces & Sagittarius (*November 23 to December 21*)   Challenging

Pisces & Capricorn (*December 22 to January 20*)   Passionate

Pisces & Aquarius (*January 21 to February 20*)   Harmonious

Pisces & Pisces (*February 21 to March 20*)   Harmonious

Miss Pisces and Her Men

She can be confident and mysterious, like Pisceans
Sharon Stone and Erykah Badu, or sweet and funny, like
Fish women Drew Barrymore and Holly Hunter.
In either case, this woman wears her heart on her sleeve and is
a hopeless romantic. Sometimes she overestimates
a partner's goodness, only to be disappointed. This sensitive
lady needs a man to appreciate her dreaminess while
providing reliability, since her emotional life is volatile.

Pisces Woman & Aries Man

Erykah Badu seeks Tito Puente.

They appreciate each other's opposite qualities, but it will take a lot of work to make this relationship last. He's basically a fiery male who goes after what he wants and rarely backs down once he's made up his mind. She's sensitive, adaptable, and impressionable, which means she changes her mind and her moods from minute to minute. They think they know how to nurture one another—at first. She thinks there's a sensitive soul hidden inside straightforward Mr. Aries but, while he can be delightful, he is not as sweet as she thinks. He thinks that Miss Pisces is a lady at sea who needs him to act as her anchor, though, in reality, sweet, gentle, and feminine Miss Pisces is quite independent. Sexually, his demanding style will clash with her softer approach, but this is one area where they can reach a positive compromise. If they don't succeed at love, they will succeed at enlightening each other. She'll encourage him to probe the deeper meaning of his actions, and he'll help her articulate the brilliant epiphanies she rarely shares with others.

Pisces Woman & Taurus Man

Nina Simone seeks James Brown.

With work, they can successfully blend her dreamy notions of romance with his practical approach to providing for a mate. The result is a humorous relationship that can last a lifetime. Miss Pisces effortlessly lets earthy Mr. Taurus into her life, and soon he's become both her confidante and comedian. The Bull man likes to take charge and make plans, and since she can be indecisive, his certainty and single-mindedness are good for her. She may appear calm and collected, but really Miss Pisces is just busy trying to understand her own turbulent emotions. He takes it personally when she gets depressed or contemplative, so if she can take time to explain how she's feeling, or at least acknowledge her dark moods, then this duo will find harmony sooner. Sexually, he's macho and straightforward, which makes her feel desired and safe. There are few conflicts here and many quiet evenings at home—enough, in fact, to last a lifetime.

Pisces Woman & Gemini Man

Michelle Shocked seeks Lenny Kravitz.

This creative pair will delight and inspire each other from the moment they meet, but they'll have to work to ground their relationship in reality. Since both signs are blessed with artistic vision, they'll do well together if both of them are in the arts. He responds to the world intellectually, with each new idea begetting dozens of new theories. She responds to things emotionally and often translates her feelings into some creative medium. While fantasy stokes their sex life, they'll have to create a relationship that works well in the real world. They love experiencing inspiring exhibits, museums, and poetry readings together, but neither one wants to handle the bill-paying and house-cleaning that are part of sharing a life. They'll both have to admit they need outside help to take care of the details neither of them wants to address. If they regard their relationship as a mystery, something they can know only half of, this couple may find themselves in an exalted state that sustains them throughout their lives.

Pisces Woman & Cancer Man

Taylor Dayne seeks Huey Lewis.

Mr. Cancer provides a steady shoulder for her to lean on. She feels she can tell him all her tales of woe and get sympathy for the problems brought on by her misguided optimism. In fact, he's touched by Miss Pisces's idealism. She appreciates that the Cancer man isn't afraid to share his emotions. Both of them need to feel needed, so they know how to be vulnerable with each other and also how to make each other feel secure. Sexually, they share evenings of poetic bliss. Mr. Cancer loves helping Miss Pisces overcome her negative mood swings. She is touched by his goodness, and she also knows just how to lift his spirits when he's feeling sad. With such a trusty mate in her life, she can tackle the world's woes without losing her unique outlook. After all, if her emotions overwhelm her, she can always lean on him for support. This sentimental pair will enjoy a spiritual, unconditional love.

Pisces Woman & Leo Man

Queen Latifah seeks Chuck D.

This fun-loving, boisterous man is the original party guy. Sensuous Miss Pisces, who doesn't like to attract attention to herself, is content to let him take center stage. He loves to see others enjoy and express themselves, and can turn an ordinary task into a rollicking good time. However, while few men are as entertaining and sweet—especially when they're in love—as Mr. Leo, she finds his egotism unnerving. But since Lady Pisces is often archetypally feminine, she appreciates his masculine bravado and may like the way he takes care of her. Ultimately, though, if they want to stay together, Mr. Leo will have to treat her with delicacy. He's comfortable with dramatic emotions, but doesn't know how to deal with her hurt silences. The romance and drama between them is there, particularly in the bedroom, but they'll have to compromise to write a happy ending to their own love story.

Pisces Woman & Virgo Man

Tracy Chapman seeks Moby.

Miss Pisces is so busy helping her friends sort through their emotions that she has no time to sort through her own. When Mr. Virgo thoughtfully points this out, she'll realize he's right, and that this practical man can help her organize her time. He's as generous to others as she is, only instead of providing a shoulder to cry on, he loans his car or tools or gives practical advice. Dreamy Miss Pisces, who cries at the slightest provocation, can help him make time for romance. His criticisms can come at the most inopportune moments, but she is quick to forgive. Even if Mr. Virgo notes that she's late for their anniversary—rather than tell her she looks stunning in her sequined dress—she will realize he's really saying that he couldn't wait to see her. These two will always find a way to make up after fights. Sexually, her moods can vary between timid and passionate, but his more direct approach blends well with hers. This is a healthy partnership, full of mutual respect and compassion.

Pisces Woman & Libra Man

Edie Brickell seeks Paul Simon.

Miss Pisces appreciates the fact that he's one of the few men capable of genuine romance. He is charmed by her empathy, the way she easily draws others out of their shells. She responds well to his romantic entreaties, but he may not be able to reach her emotionally. Mr. Libra's talkative and cerebral approach to problem solving won't always mesh with her more emotional perception of life. He'll need to learn how she thinks, since she isn't always able to clearly explain her emotions. Sexually, he likes her ephemeral and imaginative style, and they find a lot of joy in bed. These two have a fifty-fifty chance of success. Neither one of them is practical, but both enjoy fantasy and escape. Finding a consistent way—perhaps through a diplomatic third party—to handle the resentment or other details they both dislike to address is key for this couple. Commitment is all it takes for them to find the roses, rather than the thorns, of their union.

Pisces Woman & Scorpio Man

Nina Hagen seeks Simon LeBon.

The emotional and sexual rapport these two share is outstanding. He is honest, ambitious, and demanding, and he makes it clear that he needs her. She's creative and dreamy, and capable of creating a wonderful mood for love. He's touched, rather than mystified, by the way she sees only the best in others. When Mr. Scorpio's dark moods put him in a cynical funk, Miss Pisces is the kind of mate who reminds him that unconditional acts of kindness and good surprises still exist. He feels protective of her, but knows that her innate emotional intelligence means she can ultimately take care of herself. She doesn't always manage money well and at times can be too forgiving of those who take advantage of her, but Mr. Scorpio will steer her toward better judgment. Sensitive Miss Pisces will steer him even deeper into love—and into a relationship and a vision of a world that's a far better place than he had ever imagined.

Pisces Woman & Sagittarius Man

Karen Carpenter seeks Bruce Hornsby.

These two have many traits in common, but the sort of stability that a love relationship requires isn't one of them. Mr. Sagittarius is sexy, spiritual, and optimistic, but his blunt comments often hurt Miss Pisces's feelings and his tendency to change plans, though fun at first, ultimately confuses her. He finds her a fun partner in crime, but when her emotions throw her into a passive funk he doesn't know how to respond. The result is likely an argument. Sexually, these two imaginative lovers know how to fulfill one another's fantasies. However, reality for this pair can be difficult. Inspiration, for him, involves maps, passports, and a ten-destination trip around the world. When she's inspired, she has a quiet internal and emotional response that needs grounding and focus to be understood. What she needs is someone who can unearth her mysterious emotions and respond to them, not take them on the road. In turn, he needs someone who can respond to the new environments he's always seeking. They can appreciate each other deeply, but ultimately their most fruitful union might just be as friends.

Pisces Woman & Capricorn Man

Liza Minnelli seeks Rod Stewart.

This duo seems an unlikely match at first, but each provides the contrast the other so desperately needs. Miss Pisces finds this earthy man a bit predicable, but kind-hearted. He finds this sensitive woman impractical but well-meaning. It`s when she has her inevitable down-and-out moments that she`ll realize steady Mr. Capricorn can offer her a safe haven, both emotionally and materially. He will help her set boundaries around her endless efforts to please others, while she will help him better express his feelings. She`ll intuit that beneath his starched suit he has a romantic side, and her expectations will prompt him to play the ardent suitor she desires. She seduces him effortlessly, and his lust makes her feel needed and appreciated. She helps him create a sanctuary apart from the competitive world he experiences at work. While he might not write original love poems for her, he`ll work hard at memorizing love sonnets to whisper in her ear.

Pisces Woman & Aquarius Man

Neneh Cherry seeks Peter Gabriel.

Romantic Miss Pisces and the quirky Aquarian man can make a good match, but they'll have to work to achieve it. This is a highly impractical pair, as both are focused on saving the world, though in different ways. Mr. Aquarius has a detached, objective reaction to his surroundings, while Miss Pisces has an emotional, subjective response to hers. He wants to free people, while she offers a great deal of empathy. When she needs a pat on the back, he may be off rallying the troops for social justice. She'll listen when he needs to talk to someone about his next great idea, but will always be surprised by his ability to stay at arm's length from his feelings. In bed, they're both experimental and generous, and over time, they can grow close. On a day-to-day basis, though, they'll have work to do. Still, giving time to their relationship may be the best cause either could commit to, and with effort they can become passionately important to each other.

Pisces Woman & Pisces Man

Vanessa Williams seeks John Cale.

These two artistic souls understand that life is a journey marked not by material achievements but by spiritual enlightenment. In each other's company, they can either share a remarkable quest for creative growth or spend years in avoidance and denial. These two are so fine-tuned to each other's emotions and needs that they are capable of finishing each other's sentences. However, this sensitivity is both a blessing and a curse. They both need the kind of stability and encouragement that they might not find in their dreamy Pisces counterpart. Their shared tendency to see the world through rose-colored glasses means they aren't always accurate with their interpretations of others' motivations, which can lead to misunderstanding. They will benefit from a third party—someone to help them handle the bills, the cleaning, and the more difficult aspects of their relationship. Their challenge is balancing the fantasy of their romance with the demands of reality. If they pull it off, life will be dreamy for both of them.

Mr. Pisces and His Women

*He can brood seductively, like Pisceans Bruce Willis
and Rob Lowe, or appear sentimental and debonair,
like Fish men Kelsey Grammer and
Billy Crystal. While intelligent and kind, he is
often subtle. He needs a woman who believes
in and encourages him—a woman whose faith will
make him the best he can possibly be. Any
woman who provides the romance and reassurance
he needs will be rewarded, as he's
one of the most romantic men in the zodiac.*

Pisces Man & Aries Woman

Johnny Cash seeks Reba McEntire.

Both these dreamers take childlike delight in the world. They make excellent traveling companions, since assertive Miss Aries loves trailblazing and imaginative Mr. Pisces likes the journey's romance. However, the active Ram woman's upside is also her downside. Her awe-inspiring drive to succeed—in the office and in love—can beget a competitive stance that bothers this sensitive man. When he hits a dark mood, he'll need more of a shoulder to lean on than she will likely provide. If she works to detect the subtlety of his moods, and he always tries to explain them to her, they could find happiness. In the bedroom, soulful Mr. Pisces isn't used to an athletic partner like Miss Aries, but he appreciates her daring approach. Outside the bedroom, he'll have to learn to speak up to get her attention, just as she'll have to learn how to slow down to hear what he's really saying. However, the zodiac's woman warrior knows a good thing when she finds it—and if she finds herself in love with Mr. Pisces, she won't let him go.

Pisces Man & Taurus Woman

Bobby McFerrin seeks Janet Jackson.

Miss Taurus makes him remember that strong women can be sensitive too. Mr. Pisces appreciates her steady manner, her practicality, and her sensuality. Miss Taurus considers him creative, sensitive, and far more intelligent than his peers. In bed, she's as romantic as he is, and beyond the bedroom she instinctively knows how to add stability and comfort to his life. However, her emphasis on financial security makes nonmaterialistic Mr. Pisces nervous. Though she appreciates the depth of his spiritual approach to life, she can't feel safe until she feels financially secure, and she knows that this dreamy man's priorities don't always match her practical ones. If he wants to keep Miss Taurus, he'll have to back up the emotional support he gladly offers with a steady paycheck to keep the home fires burning. Their doubts about each other are unnecessary. The fact of the matter is that she is every bit as sensitive as he is. She just wants to make sure they can balance dreamy romance and secure intimacy, so the rest of their lives will remain as delightful as their promising beginnings.

Pisces Man & Gemini Woman

Lou Reed seeks Laurie Anderson.

Sociable Miss Gemini is as easily delighted—and quickly chagrined—as sensitive Mr. Pisces. He will find her wanderlust and detachment from the immediate environment surprisingly familiar. They both have an active imagination, but for her it inspires eccentric intellectualism rather than emotions and fantasies. She'll be able to accept his fickle moods, since she is subject to them as well. They often share a precise viewpoint and notice details no one else does. They'll enjoy spending time together in artistic environments like museums, bookstores, and film festivals, where their imaginations can soar and collide. To make things work out in the real world—and in the bedroom—they'll have to compromise, as Miss Gemini can turn her feelings on and off more easily than this sensitive man. With a little nurturing from her and a little focus from him, they'll be able to bring the magic to the home and hearth.

Pisces Man & Cancer Woman

James Taylor seeks Suzanne Vega.

Earnest Miss Cancer can have a soothing effect on sensitive Mr. Pisces. She intuits and sweetly addresses his moods and needs before he even tries to describe them to her—especially in bed, where their evenings together are poetic. Moody Mr. Pisces doesn't like to rest in one place for long, but with gentle Miss Cancer in his life, he re-thinks this tendency. He may find that for the first time in his life, he wants to be right where he is. These two are good for each other. Each will feel inspired to guard against their self-acknowledged and selfish tendency to sulk, and to become the available, strong partner the other needs. Though they are both very emotional, which makes for lively conversations and the occasional tearful fight, this relationship has great potential. These two will fall in love at first sight, and never take their eyes off each other.

Pisces Man & Leo Woman

Al Jarreau seeks Aimee Mann.

This outspoken, entertaining woman exudes a zest for life that refreshes Mr. Pisces, but she doesn't always provide the sensitivity or stability he needs in a full-time partner. However, if they can work out how to treat each other right, this duo can share a spiritual connection. While Miss Leo may inadvertently hurt his feelings with her blunt demands and forthright criticisms, she soon learns that his need for calm is really just his cry for comfort. She can teach the most unselfish man in the zodiac that he should put himself first now and then, while he can teach her to convert her passion for dramatic emotion into compassion for others. Her athletic approach to lovemaking may clash with his more gentle affections in bed, but since both of them like to please, they can overcome these differences. Mr. Pisces will let Miss Leo boss him around, while she'll let him move her to tears. They make an odd couple, but if they encourage each other they'll be two of the happiest oddballs around.

Pisces Man & Virgo Woman

Neil Sedaka seeks Gloria Gaynor.

This sensitive pair would never suspect they were right for each other. As the zodiac's two most selfless signs, they rarely know what's best for themselves—they're too busy doing good deeds for other people. Miss Virgo rolls up her sleeves and helps friends hammer out a practical plan, while Mr. Pisces provides loved ones with a shoulder to cry on. She gives the gift of structure, while he gives the gift of empathy. In bed, his sensitive approach to this emotionally restrained woman unlocks her hidden passions, and her earthy response to his sensitive touch makes them a good match. He pays attention to the sort of romantic details she forgets, such as candles and music to set a mood, or flowers and champagne to celebrate. Meanwhile, she's happy to oversee the unromantic details he forgets: paying the bills on time, staying fit, and remembering important events. They'll smile and introduce one another as "my better half"—and mean it.

Pisces Man & Libra Woman

Michael Bolton seeks Tiffany.

When Mr. Pisces, the zodiac's spiritual seeker, meets diplomatic Miss Libra, the result is a duo that shares a love of the arts and creativity. However, while she is inspired by creative trends in contemporary culture and stays up-to-date on everything from art shows to fashion, he sees creativity as the manifestation of man's connection to eternal spiritual mysteries. With their worldly and otherworldly sides providing contrast, they make an inspired but impractical pair. Sexually, she's romantic yet also playfully suggestive. However, he won't understand her need to discuss every issue endlessly, and she won't understand his quiet side or need for solitude. Miss Libra's optimism lifts his spirits, but Mr. Pisces's moods may drain her. They might not agree about money, as she is more materialistic. However, if they find a way around these hurdles—preferably through a diplomatic third party, since they both dislike addressing the relationship's tougher details—they can enjoy a life of aesthetic pleasures and good times.

Pisces Man & Scorpio Woman

Jon Bon Jovi seeks Grace Slick.

The experienced lady and romantic man understand one another instantly. Their emotional rapport is excellent, and resilient Miss Scorpio can teach fragile Mr. Pisces to face his emotions more directly and to prevent others from taking advantage of his big heart. She needs a loving man who will share his emotions and possessions, and unconditional Mr. Pisces delivers on both fronts. Sexually, they are one of the most compatible combinations in the zodiac, as his flexibility accommodates her demands. She is the understanding woman he needs, since she can prod him to act on his dreams without the nagging that makes him balk. He is not traditionally ambitious or materialistic, but since talented Miss Scorpio knows how to provide for herself—and will expect him to do the same—this won't hinder them. With minimal work, they can strike a perfect balance, and may want to settle down and have children together. Their quiet home will be a haven of kindness and creativity for their trusted friends to enjoy. This love is written in the stars.

Pisces Man & Sagittarius Woman

Fats Domino seeks Etta Jones.

This duo shares an interest in religion and mysticism that can either bind or separate them, depending on their age and their backgrounds. Miss Sagittarius likes athletic endeavors and philosophical debates, while Mr. Pisces is into romantic talk and sentimental poetry. She sees the world as an intellectual challenge, while he interprets the world emotionally. She passes through a thousand cities on her route to enlightenment, while he can sit perfectly still and pass through a thousand moods. They're both imaginative, flexible, dreamy people motivated by high ideals. They share less flattering characteristics as well; both can be impractical, unreliable, and self-absorbed. Sexually, their imaginative approach makes them compatible, but when it comes to day-to-day reality these two might not quite provide what the other needs. Deep friendship may be the path to enlightenment for these two philosophers.

Pisces Man & Capricorn Woman

Tone-Loc seeks Mary J. Blige.

The ultra-direct Capricorn achiever and a sensitive, romantic dreamer like Mr. Pisces make an unexpectedly dynamic duo. She can provide him with the structure he needs, while he can provide her with the romance she's too proud to admit she craves. Her goal-oriented approach to life can bring him down to earth. Miss Capricorn may tense up when she encounters his indifference to money and what she sees at times as a lack of ambition. However, if she appreciates the fact that he's one of the few men who isn't intimidated by her intelligence and success—in fact, he supports her efforts to tackle the corporate world—then their union could be a strong one. In bed, her lusty response to his romantic overtures reassures him. With the zodiac's power partner for a mate, this beatnik guy may even decide to go out in the world and slay his own dragons, rather than merely write poetry about them. They'll share a lively relationship that strikes the perfect balance between reality and romance.

Pisces Man & Aquarius Woman

Eddie Money seeks Juice Newton.

If these two idealists commit to making their relationship a priority, they can make a winning duo. Inspired by different sources, intellectual Miss Aquarius reads the newspaper while emotional Mr. Pisces interprets his dreams. It will take an outside force to kick-start their relationship, because both of them have a way of idling as people come and go in their lives. If they grow attracted, though, their friendship will serve as a foundation for love. She's drawn to his sensitivity and depth, though at times she'll have a hard time understanding his need to withdraw from the madding crowds she so enjoys. He's attracted to her warmth and intelligence, and will share her passion for humanitarian causes. In bed, she is talkative and quirky while he is suggestive and mysterious; they will amuse each other, and, over time, learn just how to please each other. He'll teach her that love can revolutionize her life. In turn, she'll teach him that romance exists in the here-and-now—not just in his dreams.

Pisces Man & Pisces Woman

Glen Miller seeks Irene Cara.

They can move each other with their kind gestures and empathy towards friends, but they'll have to pay careful attention to their own relationship for it to grow. Both Mr. and Miss Pisces have a tendency to withhold their true desires in an effort not to burden a partner, so for them to enjoy each other, they'll need to learn to better express their needs. One thing they will easily express is Pisces's legendary love of romance and fantasy. The sexual sparks between these two, combined with their willingness to try anything once, makes for memorable moments in the bedroom. On a practical level, they'll need to work extra hard to attend to the tiresome bill-paying and house-cleaning that are part of daily life since both would rather deal with lofty ideas than cold, hard facts. However, if they strike a balance between the pragmatism they need to survive and the romance that keeps love alive, they can live in nirvana.

Pisces at Home

The Pisces home is a quiet place designed to serve as a refuge and a space for meditation. Homes owned by Pisceans are filled with shiny silver accessories that lend their rooms a cool quality, soft subtle colors, and often an aquarium of colorful fish. Those born under this sign are equally comfortable in the city or the country, but behind the front door they will strive to create a romantic and otherworldly atmosphere with unusual lighting, scented candles or incense, and soothing music. They pay careful attention to tablecloths, bedding, and drapes, and often use diaphanous, shimmering fabrics that create almost aquatic effects. The Piscean bedroom may have romantic touches, like an antique bedframe, fresh flowers, or satin sheets, to set the stage for passionate scenes. If they can swing it, Pisceans will install an outdoor pool where they can float and daydream. Whether an artist's studio or a fancy country home, the Piscean dwelling emanates creativity and inspires the imagination.

Pisces Health

As night owls and fans of the glamorous life, Fish folks need to be careful to eat well and avoid a diet of salty cocktail food or late-night snacks. Those born under this sign can be prone to weight fluctuations. Pisces rules the feet, ankles, and toes, so Pisceans are susceptible to flat arches and foot pain. Neptune, which governs Pisces, affects the immune, nervous, and lymphatic systems, which means this sign is particularly sensitive to the food it eats. The Piscean body, like that of the other water signs, may retain water and will be highly sensitive to dehydration-inducing substances including alcohol, salt, and caffeine. Because Pisceans believe their mental and physical health are linked, they may experiment with holistic cures, reflexology, and therapeutic massage in order to cure their illnesses. These graceful folks enjoy ballroom dancing, as well as aquatic sports like canoeing or kayaking and—of course—swimming.

Pisces Style

While many Pisceans express themselves well through their wardrobes, they are less self-conscious about their image than those ruled by many other signs. They love night life, which is why their work clothes may differ significantly from what they wear after-hours, when they really like to dress up. On formal occasions, both male and female Pisceans favor bright, almost iridescent colors. Drawn to diaphanous taffeta, smooth strands of pearls, and shiny fabrics, Pisces women sometimes appear as if they've just emerged from the sea. The men favor slim, tailored suits, while women favor romantic, fitted items typical of the clothes designed by Pisces clothiers such as Givenchy, Perry Ellis, and Andre Courrèges. Since Pisces rules the feet, those born under this sign love fabulous shoes and will splurge on expensive pedicures. They love sandal season or, better yet, going barefoot. Their special stone is the aquamarine, and their color is a shimmery shade of turquoise reminiscent of the sea.

On the Road with Pisces

Travel is a joy for Pisceans, who love to experience the mystery of new surroundings and the romantic, escapist element of leaving town. They are drawn to a variety of getaways: vacations on the water, spiritual retreats, or travel to faraway cities with fine food, wine, and night life all appeal to this adaptive sign. Pisceans prefer luxury, but are capable of roughing it if that's part of the experience—they'll happily camp by a lake, for instance, if that's what the kids would like. They enjoy being near and in water and are drawn to seeing the world from a cruise ship, visiting beach or lake resorts, or motoring their own boat. Fish folks who seek spiritual and creative growth may choose to spend their vacation at a spiritual retreat in India, a secluded yoga center, or an artists' colony, where they can socialize with like-minded people in a meditative setting. Party-going Pisceans enjoy the zesty flavor of Marseille, Rio, or Miami, where they can lounge on the beach during the day, then rest up for an evening of dancing. Regardless of the setting they choose, they will look forward to immersing themselves in their new environment.

Pisces Entertaining

Pisceans love to create a special, romantic party environment. They enjoy hosting dressy affairs and attending to every last detail, from the carefully selected music to the oysters on the half-shell to the elegant ice sculptures. Delicious and unusual appetizers and expensive champagne served in elegant flutes characterize this sign's classy entertaining style. This approach, rather than being ostentatious, is their attempt to transport guests into an exotic environment—and keep them there as long as possible. Pisceans are conscious of how enjoyable it is to slip into another world for a few hours. They won't let guests lift a finger, and will take it personally if people don't let themselves enjoy being pampered. Fish folks will be sure to clear a space for a dance floor, since no Piscean party would be complete without one.

In the Company of Pisces

Musicians:
Erykah Badu
Harry Belafonte
Michael Bolton
Jon Bon Jovi
Edie Brickell
Irene Cara
Karen Carpenter
Johnny Cash
Tracy Chapman
Neneh Cherry
Frédéric Chopin
Nat King Cole
Roger Daltrey
Taylor Dayne
Fats Domino
Nina Hagen
George Harrison
Al Jarreau
Queen Latifah
Bobby McFerrin
Glen Miller
Liza Minnelli
Eddie Money
Lou Reed
Neil Sedaka
Nina Simone
James Taylor
Tone-Loc
Lawrence Welk
Vanessa Williams

Performers:
Desi Arnaz
Tom Arnold
Drew Barrymore
Glenn Close
Billy Crystal
Erik Estrada
Fabio
Peter Fonda
Jackie Gleason
Kelsey Grammer
Jean Harlow
Jennifer Love Hewitt
Ron Howard
Holly Hunter
Rob Lowe
William H. Macy
Rue McClanahan
Chuck Norris
Freddie Prinze, Jr.
Aidan Quinn
Tony Randall
Lynn Redgrave
Sharon Stone
Liz Taylor
Abe Vigoda
Bruce Willis

Reformers:
Alexander Graham Bell
W.E.B. DuBois
Albert Einstein
Mikhail Gorbachev
L. Ron Hubbard
James Madison
Ralph Nader
Ovid
Linus Pauling
Arthur Schopenhauer
Harriet Tubman
George Washington

Artists:
Sandro Botticelli
Frank Gehry
Winslow Homer
Spike Lee
Michelangelo
Piet Mondrian
Pierre-Auguste Renoir

Athletes:
Bonnie Blair
Michael Chang
Julius "Dr. J" Erving
Jackie Joyner-Kersee
Shannon Miller
Shaquille O'Neal
Bobby Orr
Lynn Swann

Writers:
Edward Albee
W. H. Auden
Erma Bombeck
Anthony Burgess
Ralph Ellison
Gabriel García Márquez
William Gibson
Allen Ginsberg
Wilhelm Grimm
(Brothers Grimm)
Alice Hoffman
Victor Hugo
John Irving
Jack Kerouac
Henry Wadsworth
Longfellow
Robert Lowell
Edna St. Vincent Millay
Anaïs Nin
George Plimpton
Philip Roth
John Steinbeck
John Updike
Tom Wolfe